BOUQUET OF *Blessings*™

Devotions to Delight Your Soul

The mission of CTA is

to glorify God by providing purposeful products that lift up and encourage the body of Christ!
because we love him.

www.CTAinc.com

Bouquet of Blessings™
Devotions to Delight Your Soul

by Carol Albrecht, Tammy Endres, Gail Marsh,
Pat Mitchell, Jane Wilke

Copyright © 2008 CTA, Inc.
1625 Larkin Williams Rd., Fenton, MO 63026

PRINTED IN THAILAND

BOUQUET OF *Blessings*

Think about creating a bouquet for someone you love. See yourself choosing just the right flowers from your garden. Think about framing those flowers with beautiful greenery. Consider choosing just the right vase in which to arrange it all—a vase that's exactly the right height, the right color, the right shape. Now, finally, see yourself placing the vase, bouquet and all, in the perfect spot in your friend's home or office—that one spot in which the bouquet will look as splendid and cheerful as possible.

I hope that reading the paragraph above warmed your heart. I love assembling bouquets to honor my friends, to cheer the members of my family and my office staff. And it warms my heart to receive a fresh-cut bouquet of flowers, especially when I know that someone chose them just for me.

This devotional booklet will help you explore the many blessings God has placed into your life, tying in ideas from the art of flower arranging to help explain and clarify. Those of us who wrote the devotions pray that our words will help you more fully celebrate those blessings as you worship your Lord for them!

The Garden:
Planted to Blossom

There are few things lovelier than a flower garden in bloom. Spilling over with rich colors, a well-planned and well-tended garden becomes a reflection of the love and nurture of the gardener. God has planted you in just the right place in his creation and in his church. You are rich in your own beauty and a showcase of God, our Master Gardener, at work in you.

> *I am sure of this, that he who began a good work in you will bring it to completion at the day of Jesus Christ.*
>
> *Philippians 1:6 ESV*

Blessed:
A Choice Location

*I praise you because I am fearfully
and wonderfully made; your works
are wonderful, I know that full well.*
Psalm 139:14

"Bloom where are you planted." This well-known saying often evokes smiles and creates hope, the hope of making a difference. But it can also evoke a bit of cynicism. We may wonder, "What if we're planted in the wrong place?" Gardens that flourish enjoy just the right location, a location chosen so that whatever is planted can bloom to its full potential.

Selecting the perfect location for a garden requires intentional planning and research. You want it close enough to your house so that you can tend to it faithfully. (Keep in mind another much-used saying, "Out of sight, out of mind!") You may ask yourself, "Will it be easy to water if I put it here?" and, "Is that spot too shady or too sunny?"

Gardeners also need to know what types of plants will grow and flourish in a particular kind of soil and in their specific climate. Imagine what would happen if you tried to plant the bougainvillea you saw on your vacation to Mexico in your own yard in Minnesota!

Even before God created the Garden of Eden, he had each of us in mind. He made the entire universe—his garden—with each of us specifically in his thoughts and on his heart. God knew precisely what mix of talents and gifts he would blend together so that you would bloom in a way different from anyone else. God knew what nurturing you would require, what weeding would be necessary, and what pruning would make it possible for you to branch out to your full potential. Your Lord made you to be beautiful, precious, and cherished. No one else can fill your place in his garden.

Today's verse gives us only a brief glimpse of this truth; Psalm 139 paints it much more fully. Sometime today you may want to read the entire psalm. Take in each verse, word by word.

Consider: God, who knows your every thought, word, and deed, is also the Master Gardener who planted you where you are today. He has chosen just the right spot, and he is anxious to see you bloom, reflecting the love he so graciously bestows upon you.

Lord, you are awesome in wonder! Help me bloom where you have planted me! Amen.

Blessed:
Preparing to Plant

‹‐◦◦◦─›

*I pray that you, being rooted and
established in love, may have power,
together with all the saints, to grasp
how wide and long and high and
deep is the love of Christ.*

Ephesians 3:17–18

God has chosen just the right spot in which to
plant you. And you may be sure that he has carefully prepared the soil.

Good gardeners know the secret to growing
healthy plants is having healthy soil—soil that
allows roots to reach deep to absorb the water
and nutrients that allow plants to thrive.
Sometimes gardeners find that a "perfect spot"
from an artistic perspective offers only rock-hard
soil or a permanent bed of weeds.

In the parable of the sower (Matthew 13:1–9;
Mark 4:1–12; Luke 8:4–8) Jesus contrasts unpro-
ductive ground with good soil. If the soil is too
hard, the seed will not penetrate and can be
stolen by birds. If the soil is too rocky, the roots
will grow quickly but end up being shallow. If the
seed falls among thorns or weeds, the plants will
be choked.

Jesus did not intend this parable to be a lesson on farming. Rather, he described the Word of God sown into human hearts. In light of that, consider your own life. What might be preventing the seed of God's Word from fully taking root in you? Is anything stealing your joy or keeping you from grasping "how wide and long and high and deep is the love of Christ" (Ephesians 3:18)?

Take heart, for preparing the soil is not up to you; it's up to the gardener. God, the Master Gardener, has turned the soil of your heart over and removed the rocks and weeds of sin through the death and resurrection of his very own Son, Jesus Christ. The "living water" of the Holy Spirit (John 7:37–39) will penetrate deeply and will fully circulate. And if the rocks and thorns reappear, our Gardener patiently removes them, again and again, forgiving our sins at the cross of Jesus and giving us a fresh start, with mercies new every morning.

Lord Jesus, do your holy work in me. May I soak in the full measure of the Spirit as your Word touches my heart. May the world see Jesus in me! Amen.

Blessed:
Balanced and
Blooming

*Let us hold unswervingly to the hope
we profess, for he who promised is
faithful. And let us consider how we
may spur one another on toward love
and good deeds.*

Hebrews 10:23–24

God's garden is sprouting and growing! No one
watched as he planned and prepared to plant, but
the results will soon be visible for all to see.

Gardeners spend a great deal of time figuring out
what the garden will look like as summer deep-
ens. Will it be formal and orderly, or will it appear
more casual, with sweeping curves and irregular
clumps? Which plants should go where to provide
the right balance of height? What plants will fill
the garden with color during the growing season,
each blooming at a different time? And how might
some features be arranged to attract butterflies
and bees?

Choosing what to plant is a bit like putting friends
together. Can you point to friends who have
helped you blossom, grow, and flourish? These
friends may differ from you in many ways, but

your friendships fit together to create an artful masterpiece.

Yet, the opposite can also be true. It might look wonderful to plant flowers around the base of that large, mature tree you've always loved, but the intense competition for moisture and nutrients can keep the flowers from blooming to their full potential. Did you know that placing plants too close together can actually stop some of them from growing?

Who in your circle of friends provides a sense of balance and helps you thrive? Who complements you as a companion—not overwhelming you, but supporting you? Who is there to listen, to care, and to protect? On the other end of the spectrum, is there someone who is actually attracting the pests and introducing spiritual diseases that will stunt your growth or threaten to destroy you?

Take heart as you reread Hebrews 10:23–24. Then ask Jesus to bring into your life the kinds of companionship that will spur you on to "love and good deeds."

Lord Jesus, make me an encourager *to* others, even as you encourage me *through* others. Amen.

Blessed:
Tenderly Nourished

*Seek first his kingdom and his
righteousness, and all these things
will be given to you as well. Therefore
do not worry about tomorrow, for
tomorrow will worry about itself. Each
day has enough trouble of its own.*
Matthew 6:33–34

Imagine your garden at the height of summer—a
mosaic of color, a masterpiece of design! In fact,
you are in contention for the Garden of the Year
Award. So, now you can sit back and simply
enjoy the beauty and fame, right? No. Gardens
need tending. Garden work is never done!

Gardeners attend all season long to the nutrients
their plants need. Many of these can be found in
the air, water, and the soil itself. The soil must be
aerated. Deep watering is necessary for the good
of the plants' roots. And there's always the likeli-
hood that plant food or fertilizer will boost the
intensity of the color and the number of blooms.

On the flip side, gardeners take away as well as
add—always for the good of the garden. Consider
weeds, those nasty pests that thrive on the very
water and nutrients flowers and vegetables need.

Weeds can be tricky—some actually flower and look like the plants you are trying to grow! And while some have shallow roots that can be easily pulled by hand, others have root systems that reach deep below the surface, allowing weeds to spring up in the most unexpected places. Gardeners must dig deep to destroy them.

With this in mind, reflect: Are there weeds in the garden of your life that threaten to overwhelm you? Are troubles threatening to choke you? Or are they stealing your sense of balance and peace? Are you in need of richer spiritual nutrients?

If any of this describes you today, look to the Master Gardener, who continues to tend to his garden, to care for you personally. Notice the ways in which he uses his Word to help you recognize the weeds of sin. Praise him that as you confess these sins, he forgives and removes them for Jesus' sake. Receive his Word with humility and faith as it makes your faith flourish.

With all this in mind, consider today how blessed you truly are as you thrive in the garden of your God!

Father, you bathe me in Son Light each day. May I grow strong and flourish in your love. Amen.

Blessed:
Expressing Christ's Love

But to each one of us grace has been given as Christ apportioned it . . . to prepare God's people for works of service, so that the body of Christ may be built up.

Ephesians 4:7, 12

Bouquets of freshly cut flowers rarely fail to bring a smile. Without words, they can fill a need. Without words, they can touch a heart. Without words, they can express love.

Gardening calls for a great deal of hard work, but it is also truly a labor of love. A gardener receives ample reward for her efforts when she is able to share the harvest with others. A flower garden offers beauty and delight; a vegetable garden, food and sustenance.

Never doubt that God labors over you in love! You are his masterpiece, and he intends to bless others through you. He is constantly tending you in his garden—sometimes shifting you from one place to another, sometimes pruning you so that your blooms can grow more vibrant in color.

Continually, he waters you. Often he plucks out weeds that threaten to choke you. And as you begin to blossom, he gives you the opportunity to respond to his tender care and love by reflecting that love to others.

Ephesians 4 points us to an incredible, eternal truth: When we were still sinners, God heaped his grace upon us. He sent his own Son to bear the ultimate punishment—death—not for his own sin, but for your sin and mine. Jesus Christ destroyed the power of everything that threatened to destroy us—even death itself. For Jesus' sake, God forgives us and sustains us. How can we not respond in love to his tender care?

As the Master Gardener, God had a great purpose in planting you where you are today. Just as a bouquet of flowers becomes an expression of love and care when shared with others, your gifts of serving and caring become an expression of God's love in the lives of others. Without words, you fill a need. Without words, you touch hearts. Without words, you express love.

Lord Jesus, you are the Master Gardener. Place me where you will and work in me so that I may truly bloom where I am planted. Amen.

The Garden of Gratitude

Serve one another in love.
Galatians 5:13

I am sure of this, that he who began a good work in you will bring it to completion at the day of Jesus Christ.
Philippians 1:6 ESV

Whether you eat or drink or whatever you do, do it all for the glory of God. . . . Follow the example of Christ.
1 Corinthians 10:31; 11:1

The Flowers:
Physical Blessings

Wherever God makes flowers bloom, praises rise to heaven. Whenever he floods our lives with blessings, we, too, respond in songs of praise!

Flowers appear on the earth;
the season of singing has come.
                    Song of Songs 2:12

Blessed:
A Bouquet
of Friends

A friend loves at all times.

Proverbs 17:17

God has uniquely designed each person he has brought into your life. Some bring balance, while others infuse vibrancy, bring focus with pizzazz, or fill in empty spaces with simplicity. Together, you make a brilliant bouquet. Each person comes to you, intended as a blessing from your Lord.

Consider these examples:

Do you know Rose? Rose buds begin tightly closed and then slowly open up to reveal individual layers of petals that lead deeper to the flower's center. Is there someone in your life who is difficult to get to know? Don't grow weary in the waiting. She will bless you as she unfolds in God's time. As God reveals his mysteries to your "Rose," she will become increasingly more beautiful.

Do you know Lily? Lily of the Valley, I mean? The valley is a place of growth, but it is often also a place of suffering. Romans 5:3–5 promises blessings to those who persevere in suffering: "We also rejoice in our sufferings, because we know

that suffering produces perseverance; perseverance, character; and character, hope. And hope
does not disappoint us, because God has poured
out his love into our hearts by the Holy Spirit." Yet
when trials are severe or persistent, rejoicing isn't
so easy. Perhaps God is inviting you to come
alongside your "Lily" to encourage her!

Do you know Forget-Me-Not? Forget-me-nots
have clusters of small blue flowers—unforgettably
beautiful! Have you said good-bye to someone
you'll never forget? Perhaps a family member has
gone on to be with the Lord or a dear friend has
moved far away. Their absence leaves you feeling
blue, and yet the beauty of your relationship
remains. If so, continue to praise your generous
Lord for that treasured friend. Join the psalmist in
worship: "Bless the LORD, O my soul, and forget
not all his benefits" (Psalm 103:2 ESV).

**Lord, I am so thankful for the bouquet of
relationships you use to beautify my life.
Help me to add beauty
to the lives I touch.
Amen.**

Blessed:
A Bouquet of Benefits

---

*Praise the LORD, O my soul; all my
inmost being, praise his holy name. . . .
Forget not all his benefits.*

Psalm 103:1–2

"I come to the garden alone,
While the dew is still on the roses;
And the voice I hear, falling on my ear,
The Son of God discloses."

C. Austin Miles wrote these opening words of
"In the Garden" nearly two centuries ago. As he
thought about walking and talking with Jesus,
he envisioned roses.

Roses of various colors have come to communi-
cate different meanings. If we have eyes to see
and hearts to understand, each color can represent blessings that come to us from God through
his church, other believers in the body of Christ.
As the fruit and gifts of the Spirit operate in us
and in our brothers and sisters in Jesus, God
encourages and strengthens us.

Red roses symbolize love, a fruit of the Spirit.
We see Christ's love for us in his blessing us with
faithful pastors who proclaim God's Word to us
and who walk with us in the milestone times of
our lives. Week by week, our pastors remind us

that like the red rose, the blood shed by Jesus expresses his unconditional and eternal love for us and his full pardon for all our sins.

Pink roses symbolize grace and elegance. What a blessing when friends in Christ's church have and use gifts of hospitality. They create an atmosphere of warmth and beauty. These people bless us, encourage us, and build us up.

White roses represent purity, honor, and reverence. We might think of the intercessors in our church whenever we see white roses. Their prayer lives are deep, and they take our needs to the throne room of heaven with humility and faithfulness.

Many people see orange roses as communicating enthusiasm. Who has (or needs!) more enthusiasm than nursery and youth workers who mentor young believers and fill them with zeal to spread the Gospel?!

Lord Jesus, the people of my congregation come to me as true blessings from you! Help me cherish them, lift them up in prayer, and praise you for them. Amen.

Blessed:
A Bouquet of Praise

*How lovely is your dwelling place,
O LORD of hosts! My soul longs, yes,
faints for the courts of the LORD; my heart
and flesh sing for joy to the living God.*
Psalm 84:1–2 ESV

We don't stop often enough to thank God for his blessing of creativity. But think about how that blessing guides and shapes our worship. Think about how it evokes our praise! For the artist and the musician, expression is like breathing out beauty. For those who see, hear, and are guided in our worship by works of art and music, impression is like breathing in revelation.

But thanks be to God, who in Christ always leads us in triumphal procession, and through us spreads the fragrance of the knowledge of him everywhere.

2 Corinthians 2:14 ESV

Like the aroma of flowers in a garden, the knowledge of God is a fragrance that spreads everywhere—at least in part through the creativity of artisans, musicians, and many other artists:

• Paintings and sculptures of biblical characters fill museums and churches.

- Concert halls and church services ring with the harmonies of symphonies and choirs.

Let all the heavens resound with his name;
Let all the earth sing his glory and fame.
Ocean and mountain, stream, forest,
  and flower
Echo his praises and tell of his power.

("Blessing and Honor and Glory and Power," Horatius Bonar)

Sacred music. Sacred art. All the work of Christian artists blesses us. But our Lord, ever generous, gives even more: music to lighten our day as we work or drive; paintings and plays that send our spirits soaring or set our minds to thinking; sculptures that brighten our homes; books that lift our hearts.

All of these are blessings from God, flowers of blessing that bring us to our knees in praise!

Lord, help me see the beautiful gifts you have placed all around me for my enjoyment and stimulation. Help me to express your love and beauty to others with care and creativity. Amen.

Blessed:
A Bouquet
of Precious Memories

*The grass withers and the flowers fall,
but the word of our God stands forever.*
Isaiah 40:8

My daughter recently attended her high school
prom. We called our local florist to order the
young man's boutonniere and then went to pick it
up on the big day. I overheard the woman making
flower arrangements in the back ask if this was
the last weekend of proms. Her co-worker, the
clerk waiting on my daughter and me, answered
"Yes," with a sigh of relief. "Next weekend is
Mother's Day," she explained to us, "and we're so
busy putting together bouquets for that, it would
nearly kill us to have to fill orders for another
prom, too!"

Nearly every society in history has made special
occasions more memorable by adding flowers. A
bride chooses just the right combination of blossoms for her wedding bouquet. A college student
attending an out-of-state university sends roses to
his hometown sweetheart on Valentine's Day. On
New Year's Day, we sit glued to our television
sets, marveling at the floats in the Rose Parade—
made entirely of vibrant and delicate flowers.

The giving and receiving of flowers also marks the less joyful occasions of our lives, making them somehow more bearable. A newly married husband brings his young wife flowers after their first spat. We stop by the hospital gift shop to buy flowers for an ailing friend. We grieve the loss of loved ones and celebrate their going home to be with Jesus, all by giving and receiving flowers.

The flowers we give and receive on memorable occasions like these don't last very long. But we carry the lessons God teaches us in them for the rest of our lives.

The grass withers. Flower petals fall. We ourselves walk the earth for only a few short years. Yet, our Lord uses those years and every experience in them to bless us if we but let him touch, strengthen, confront, and comfort us in his Word of life!

Lord, help me reflect right now on the everyday moments of my life. Then help me recall the highest high points and the deepest low points. Help me see you standing beside me through it all, forgiving me and shaping me in Christlikeness through each experience, as you pour your Word into my heart. Amen.

Blessed:
A Bouquet of Provision

[Jesus said,] "And why do you worry?"

Matthew 6:28

Lily liked playing soccer and could scale up a tree like a monkey. But what she loved the most was dancing. Lily lived with her mom in a small apartment. They didn't have much money, but her mom had managed to scrape up a few extra dollars so Lily could take dance lessons. Lily twirled and swirled in front of the mirror week after week, enjoying every moment of it.

One week, the teacher announced an upcoming dance recital. Leotards and tutus, ordered specially for the occasion, would help all the girls to look alike. Lily's mom was quiet on the way home, not knowing how she could possibly afford the outfit her daughter wanted. Lily sensed her mom's worry and said with enthusiasm, "Don't worry, Mama, Jesus will help." They prayed a simple prayer together.

Weeks passed, and Lily's mom grew more concerned each day. But Lily just played soccer, climbed trees, and practiced her dance routine in front of the mirror. One day, while talking with her friend Rose, Lily's mom mentioned her concern. Rose said, "No problem! Daisy has a white leotard from her snowflake recital. It could be dyed the color Lily needs, and we can sew sequins on the legs to match the custom-made outfit."

Lily was the star of the show, at least in her mom's eyes. In the car on the way home Lily's mom said, "We must remember to thank Jesus for helping us."

"Don't worry, Mama," Lily said, "I already did."

> *[Jesus said,] "And why do you worry about clothes? See how the lilies of the field grow. They do not labor or spin. Yet I tell you that not even Solomon in all his splendor was dressed like one of these. . . . So do not worry, saying, 'What shall we eat?' or 'What shall we drink?' or 'What shall we wear?' For the pagans run after all these things, and your heavenly Father knows that you need them. But seek first his kingdom and his righteousness, and all these things will be given to you as well."*
> Matthew 6:28–33

Lord, forgive my sinful and foolish worries. Help me trust your promise to provide. Amen.

Blossoms
of Peace

May the God of hope fill you with all joy and peace as you trust in him, so that you may overflow with hope by the power of the Holy Spirit.

Romans 15:13

Know this love that surpasses knowledge— that you may be filled to the measure of all the fullness of God.

Ephesians 3:19

This is my prayer: that your love may abound more and more.

Philippians 1:9

The Greenery:
Spiritual Blessings

Beautiful all by themselves, flowers bring even more delight when we add greenery to frame a bouquet. Similarly, and to our delight, our Savior adds his eternal, spiritual "greenery" to the physical blessings we receive from him.

> *Praise the LORD, O my soul,*
> *and forget not all his benefits—*
> *who forgives all your sins . . .*
> *and crowns you with love and*
> *compassion.*
>
> *Psalm 103:2–4*

Blessed:
Forgiveness

Forgive as the Lord forgave you.
Colossians 3:13

We're ready to give our floral arrangement shape, depth, and texture. We choose the greenery carefully, putting leaves in just the right places, hiding a misshapen bud, framing a vivid blossom.

Perhaps that's the way God adds "greenery" to our lives. Seeing the uniqueness of each of his daughters, he carefully weaves in spiritual qualities we need, making our lives much more beautiful—and beautiful for all eternity!

What spiritual blessing does he bring to our bouquet? Maybe he first whispers, "You need to learn forgiveness." And he might choose to symbolize it with yarrow. A tough little plant with feathery leaves and yellow flowers, yarrow has been used since ancient times for healing. Its leaves stop bleeding when held against a wound. Similarly, forgiveness stops the bleeding too, the bleeding of brokenness and hate.

Forgiveness is foreign to our human nature; revenge is more to our liking. Yet Jesus asks us to forgive. In fact, he specifically addresses that issue in the Lord's Prayer.

Not that it's easy. In the nasty circumstances of life—divorce, estrangement, lies, betrayal, abuse—forgiveness comes much harder.

In times like that, forgiveness comes only as we see Jesus—betrayed, mocked, bleeding, dying—all this for us! As his forgiveness floods into our lives, we worship in sweet relief.

Then, hearing him praying from Calvary for his enemies, we begin to see the way to let go of bitterness ourselves. Jesus forgave aloud so we would understand that no one earns forgiveness. No one is sorry enough or does enough to make up for their offenses.

Instead, God's forgiveness is a gift—a pure, simple gift of love that releases the offender. Receiving that gift, that awesome gift, frees us from the heavy load of guilt, and we can ask God sincerely for his grace to forgive others and for the peace that comes when we forgive.

Our Father-Gardener tucks his yarrow gently into our lives, nestling it among the blooms. See its soft leaves brush the flowers, making them appear brighter against its muted green?

Lord, your forgiveness, quiet and deep, refreshes my heart. Point me to the cross, and give me a forgiving heart. Amen.

Blessed:
Patience

*Be patient, then, brothers, until the
Lord's coming.*

James 5:7

Sit back, relax, and wait. Wait for what? An
answer to prayer? Money to pay bills? Better
health? Here comes the Gardener, carrying long
green fronds, ready to enhance the blossoms of
our lives with iris leaves of patience.

Irises put out long slim leaves. Cut an iris, mow
over it, and it will simply send up more shoots. A
late-season frost that makes other plants struggle
usually won't faze a bed of irises. The roots keep
right on sprouting more leaves. Patience is something like those leaves. It's a quiet, unobtrusive
virtue that simply will not quit.

Our Lord exercises patience with us day by day.
He bears with us, forgiving us for repeated sins,
soothing our hurts, waiting for our return when
we stray. 1 Timothy 1:16 tells us that Jesus has
unlimited patience as he works to win over those
who don't know or trust in him as their Savior.

The Master Gardener knows that we need
patience, too. Without it, life's little irritations

easily blow up into disasters, hurting and destroying relationships unless we respond in patience.

Patience is especially valuable when we're faced with problems that seem insurmountable. We may wring our hands, demanding answers from God, when our lives fall into disarray. But our Lord loves us even then. In patience, he forgives our lack of trust, as he reminds us that he doesn't operate on our time schedule.

Everything he does, he does for his glory and our good. Trials are meant to lead us to the Father, who longs to carry our burdens. As we trust him, iris leaves of patience grace our lives.

As our Gardener inserts an iris leaf here, another there in our bouquet, he reminds us that we have a special reason to be patient. He has promised to take us home to live with him. Maybe tomorrow, maybe next week. Maybe it won't happen for years. Though we wait, while we wait, we trust.

My Savior, I seem to have plenty of opportunities to practice patience! Give me joy and endurance, trusting you are at work in me and in those challenging circumstances I face.
Amen.

Blessed:
Joy

*May the God of all hope fill you
with all joy and peace as you trust
in him, so that you may overflow
with hope by the power of the Holy Spirit.*
Romans 15:13

The Gardener is returning, waving large branches in both hands. Listen! He's singing. This must be some special greenery for our bouquet!

As he comes closer, we recognize the branches. They are palm fronds, large and wide, all ready for our arrangement. Maybe the Gardener chose them to remind us of that first Palm Sunday when people lined the street, singing praises to Jesus, calling him King. A happy day!

Or maybe he chose them because a strong central stem supports the willowy fronds. Like those fronds, our joy remains strong because it is connected to Jesus and to his love for us. By his death on the cross, he removed the curse of sin. We're freed from its guilt, released from the shame and fears sin brings into every life. Unconditional forgiveness and peace with God are ours forever! Sing, oh soul, sing for joy!

Joy pops out everywhere, in the way we share our lives, our gifts, and our talents. It bubbles into each corner, touching others, reverberating back to God. You can't easily hide a palm branch, and you can't easily hide joy.

Are you struggling with the day-to-day annoyances of life? Add a little palm-branch joy. Are you weary or troubled by a more serious, long-term problem? The Master Gardener wants to plant joy in your heart. He wants it to sprout such deep roots that no trouble or challenge can destroy it. He wants to give you the kind of true joy that springs from a heart that trusts God every step of the way, in good times and bad.

Problems can't ruin godly joy, and obstacles can't quell it. That's because our joy is heaven-focused, not tied to this earth. Joy looks ahead in hope to the eternal home that awaits us, beyond the confines of time and space.

Lord, sink your "palm branch" of joy deep into the water of faith in my heart. I need joy, *your* joy! May my life shout hosanna to my Savior-King! Amen.

Blessed: Love

We love because he first loved us.
1 John 4:19

Greenery has definitely enhanced our bouquet, but there's still something missing. We spot an imperfect stem here, a drooping flower there. We need something to cover the flaws in our bouquet.

Wait—over there—yards and yards of ivy, twisted, circling, each chiseled leaf shining like a small green gem. Yes, ivy will work, just as the ivy of love also works wonders in our lives.

Since God is eternal and God is love, love has been around a long time, in fact, forever! Throughout both the Old Testament and the New, God describes himself as all love, all goodness. That pure, eternal love sent God's Son to earth to suffer and die for us. Christ's perfect love, perfect life lived in our place, and perfect death for our sins combined to save imperfect humans.

Once we experience the love of Jesus as a personal love, it changes us. Bathed in love, we're compelled to pass it on. Jesus' love becomes a blessing—spreading, surrounding over and around everyone we meet.

Perhaps because it's such an important virtue, Jesus stresses again and again how much we need leaves of love in our life. We're told in Scripture that love builds up; faith shows itself through love. Has someone trampled your feelings? Respond in love. Is a neighbor hurting, angry? Snip off an ivy leaf of love and share it with her.

Love heals and soothes by covering up other's sins. Instead of letting another's failings build a wall, those who know Christ's love can let love becomes a bridge. Knowing Jesus loves us enables us to love others, no matter what they've done to hurt us. We can leave judgment to God. Love refuses to criticize or condemn. It simply encircles a hurting heart.

Love is so important in the Christian life that the entire chapter of 1 Corinthians 13 describes it in minute detail. There we learn that love—self-giving, self-forgetting love—will never end. It will be forever, as it is right now, the language of heaven.

Lord Jesus, wind your love through every facet of my life. Let it cover my imperfections and then work in me so that my love mirrors your own—especially as I befriend those who hurt me. Amen.

Blessed:
Faith

*Now faith is being sure of what
we hope for and certain of what
we do not see.*

Hebrews 11:1

The greenery of forgiveness, patience, joy, and love have perked our bouquet right up! Still, our arrangement could use some sturdy greenery to support the whole. So even now, the Master Gardener is adding a finishing touch: pungent boughs of fir—faith—that nestle into the last remaining spaces in our bouquet.

Like forgiveness, joy, and the other spiritual blessings we have explored this week, faith flows from God as his gift to us. Faith takes us beyond ourselves, past today, over the bumps of tomorrow, all the way through and beyond life on this earth. When we live in the light of Jesus' resurrection, we are also certain of God's gift of eternal life to us—individually and personally.

Our Lord urges us to cultivate the faith he has given us by spending time in his Word and in prayer. Like the pine tree, which stays green all winter, established faith makes perseverance possible. It gives us a stick-to-it attitude that stubbornly persists, even when doubt pounds on the door and life throws stones.

One more thing about faith. Just as a branch from a fir tree has several smaller branches growing out from it, our faith is never alone. Faith and works of love always go together. Faith propels us to action. Look around you. There are needy people everywhere—people broken in body and spirit, just waiting for the pine bough of faith and good deeds God has planned for you to do.

Share it! Don't keep that fir branch to yourself; it's meant to be passed around! Let others see the long needles of faith that give you hope and invite them to add some branches to their lives, too.

Lord, let all the other spiritual blessings you have worked in my life shine in beauty against the faith you have given. Then show me how to share my faith with others. Amen.

Resplendent in Love

We love because he first loved us.
1 John 4:19

Love each other as I [Jesus] have loved you.
John 15:12

Love is patient, love is kind. It does not envy, it does not boast, it is not proud. It is not rude, it is not self-seeking, it is not easily angered, it keeps no record of wrongs. Love does not delight in evil but rejoices with the truth. It always protects, always trusts, always hopes, always perseveres.
1 Corinthians 13:4–7

The Vase:

Uniquely Me

It can be tall and slender, or short and sturdy. It can be fashioned from clay or studded with precious jewels. It can be as small as your thumb, or large enough to hold a flowering tree. In the end, every vase has the same purpose— to hold the floral creation fashioned by the gentle, caring fingers of our Creator-God!

Your hands shaped me and made me.
Job 10:8

Blessed:
Shaped to Display
God's Glory

*We are the clay, you are the potter;
we are all the work of your hand.*
Isaiah 64:8

I couldn't help myself. I just had to smile as I
removed the layers of packing paper and tenderly
withdrew my great-grandmother's flower vase.
The breath that I'd unconsciously been holding
came out in a sigh of relief. The vase survived my
U-Haul trip across the country.

With gratitude and weary satisfaction, I sat down
for the first time in hours and looked at the vase.
I wiped away a tear as I whispered, "Thanks,
Lord, for seeing that the vase survived my trip."

And I survived it, too, I pondered, as I placed the
vase on the kitchen table. Even though, like that
heirloom vase, I bear the marks of life's hard
knocks, I'm ready for God—who is forever faithful—to fill me with his beauty so others will see
his wonderful grace toward them!

Scripture sometimes refers to a vase, or pot, as
it describes God's relationship with his believers.
Molded and shaped by the Creator's hand, you

have been fashioned for his service. And your life's purpose involves something much more important than displaying floral arrangements.

Picture yourself as a vase into which God has poured out his abundant love. You have been touched by the Potter's—God's—own creative hand. Through good times and not-so-good times, your heavenly Father is gently molding and shaping you into just the right form—perfectly fashioning you for his purposes. What is your purpose? To display the glorious bouquet of God's blessings.

Your life has eternal significance. It will ultimately impact the generations that will come after you. How? As you display the grace of God in your day-to-day actions and words, co-workers will be drawn to Christ's love. As you model forgiveness in your family and neighborhood, young and old will see your Savior's love in action. When you tell about the blessings in your life, you will give God glory. And the Potter will most certainly smile!

Lord Jesus, may my life testify to your love and beauty, and may I bring you joy as I live to honor you. Amen.

Blessed:
Shaped to Contain
the Water of Life

---

*[Jesus said,] "If anyone is thirsty,
let him come to me and drink."*
                    John 7:37

For weeks I'd planned a get-together for my
neighbors, a time to get to know the people to
whom I waved as I sped off to work and retrieved
my mail from the box at the curb.

Everything was ready as I walked around one last
time—or so I thought. Then I saw that every
flower in every vase I had staged all around the
house was drooping!

I took a closer look and saw the water level—or
rather, the lack of a water level. In my hurry to
arrange each bouquet, I'd forgotten the most
important thing—water!

I hurried the bouquets into the kitchen and dis-
mantled them. Holding the bottom of the stems
under water, I quickly cut a half inch off the end
of each and placed them into vases now filled
with water. By the time I'd showered and
changed, the flowers had begun to perk up. Water
indeed has life-renewing, life-sustaining power!

The Bible mentions water over and over again. Sometimes, water is simply water. Quite often, though, Scripture uses water as a picture of the Holy Spirit. Consider John 7:37–38, which records Christ's own words:

> *If anyone is thirsty, let him come to me and drink. Whoever believes in me, as the Scripture has said, streams of living water will flow from within him.*

The thirst Jesus mentions here is so much more than physical thirst. It's the longing for relief from all the hurt sin has brought into our world. It's the longing for a personal conflict to finally end. It's the soul's cry for justice or an aching body's plea for a peaceful night's rest. Most of all, it's the guilt-ridden heart, wondering if God will really forgive—again. That's thirst. Real thirst.

Did you catch Jesus' promise? Those "streams of living water" are the Holy Spirit. The Spirit stands ready to quench your desert-dry soul. While God does not author life's troubles—job loss, divorce, illness—he intends that our trials drive us to his Word. And it is there that the Spirit pours out his life-giving, life-sustaining power.

Lord, fill me with your Spirit. Let the water of life restore my hope and bring peace, healing, and strength. Let me bloom again! Amen.

Blessed:
Shaped to Be
a Blessing

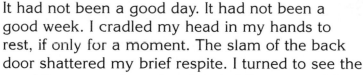

*I will bless you; . . . and you will be
a blessing.*

Genesis 12:2

It had not been a good day. It had not been a
good week. I cradled my head in my hands to
rest, if only for a moment. The slam of the back
door shattered my brief respite. I turned to see the
sparkling eyes of my tow-headed four-year-old.
"For you, Mom," she said. The dandelions
clenched in my little girl's fist danced toward
my face. "I picked bunches!"

She surely had! Following the bouncing curls to
the porch, I saw the biggest pile of dandelions I'd
ever seen! We proceeded to fill every vase and
even five water glasses with the golden beauties.
As I made a mental note to add weed spray to the
shopping list, my little girl grabbed my hand. She
insisted that I sit with her in the middle of the living room. "See? You can see flowers no matter
where you look!" she announced. Scooting
around with her, in a complete circle on the
rug, I saw that she was right.

Suddenly the entire room looked festive. Alive. Even hopeful. I continued to sit and consider the dandelions long after "Goldilocks" skipped off to find other wonders in her world. As I looked at the flowers, God spoke to my heart. He seemed to be saying words similar to those he first spoke to Abram, in Genesis 12:2: "I will bless you; . . . and you will be a blessing."

The dandelions were certainly a blessing for my child, and she, in turn, was a blessing to me. With a repentant heart, I asked my Lord to forgive me for my failure to trust him with my life's struggles. When I could not see answers to my problems, I'd forgotten that God always has in mind what's best for me. He wants to bless me—from his abundance—and then I can, in turn, be a blessing to others.

I learned important lessons that day. For one thing, dandelion flowers can survive for a very long time in a vase inside the house. But most important, I began to see that if my Savior could lift my spirits through a child's flowering weeds, he could certainly work through me to be a blessing to others.

Lord Jesus, you've blessed me so! Make me a blessing to others. Amen.

Blessed:
Shaped to Smile at God

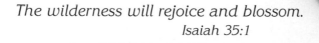

The wilderness will rejoice and blossom.
Isaiah 35:1

My grandmother loved her garden. She grew vegetables out of necessity, but she grew flowers for sheer delight. She spoke about her flowers as if they were children—dearly loved and tenderly cared for. Grandma always displayed a sure confidence about her flowers—expecting glorious blooms without question, even long before small buds began to peek through the green foliage.

Grandmother raised nine children during the bleak years following the Great Depression. She lost her parents and dear husband at an early age and found strength to manage three farms for decades following their deaths. One day in her garden, among her flowers, she helped me discover the source of her strength.

Always asking questions, I wondered aloud about her flowers. "Do all plants bloom? Why do they bloom, Grandma?"

Bending over a riotous clump of daisies, she poked at a particularly tall, bright blossom and said, "Plants bloom because that's what God made them to do. Just look at the flowers! See how their faces look up to the sky? They are smiling at God! They smile every day, thanking him for life and thanking him for his blessings of sunshine and rain."

Smiling at God. Much like her flowers, Grandma's soul smiled through the days bright with promise, as well as challenging days filled with hardship and grief. She did it because that's what God created enabled her to do. For Grandma, living a life of praise did not depend upon her circumstances, but upon her God.

As Isaiah 35 begins, the prophet paints a picture describing a hopeful life, a life filled with thanksgiving and praise, a life lived by God's people:

> *The desert and the parched land will be glad; the wilderness will rejoice and blossom. Like the crocus, it will burst into bloom; it will rejoice greatly and shout for joy.*
> Isaiah 35:1–2

Lord, help me smile at you with childlike trust, no matter what comes my way today. May I face everything with faith-filled certainty in your care, love, and forgiveness for me in Christ my Savior. Amen.

Blessed:
Shaped to Support

Carry each other's burdens.
Galatians 6:2

It came to be known affectionately as "The Friendship Vase." The vase itself was nothing special. It was pretty, but I wouldn't call it beautiful. It was serviceable, more than anything else, and sturdy, too.

My neighbor originally received the vase filled with pink roses on the day her first child was born—a girl! When their next-door neighbor, Mr. Knowles' 89-year-old wife, went home to heaven, the vase was delivered to the Knowles home. This time it held greenery and a single lily picked from the garden. The lily reminded our grieving friend of Christ's resurrection.

Over the years, the vase made its way around our neighborhood. It welcomed newlyweds to their first home, presided over anniversaries, graced the annual block party picnic table, and was once rescued from the garage sale of a newcomer who didn't yet realize its importance within our little community.

On the day I received the vase, it was filled with peonies. The spring weather had warmed to feel more like summer. Memorial Day was just around the corner, and that meant my annual trek to the cemetery to place flowers at family grave sites. I wondered how soon I would join them. A serious medical diagnosis had come as quite a shock.

Cocooned inside my home with fears and "what ifs" skipping inside my brain, I hardly noticed the doorbell ring. And then I saw "The Friendship Vase" filled with flowers. "You are not alone," the vase seemed to say. "You have a community of people who love you and will pray for you."

"The Friendship Vase" reminds me of the life God has given to each of his children. He has filled our lives with his abundant blessings. And what's more, he helps us share our blessings with the people he places in our lives.

God fills us up with love, and then he helps us fill the lives of others—with acts of love, words of grace, and whispers of encouragement.

Lord Jesus, you carried the burden of my sin to your cross. Help me more consistently see ways to lift the burdens of those around me. Amen.

Shaped by God in Grace

[The potter] was working at his wheel. And the vessel he was making of clay was spoiled in the potter's hand, and he reworked it into another vessel. . . . Then the word of the LORD came to me: "O house of Israel, can I not do with you as this potter has done? declares the LORD. Behold, like the clay in the potter's hand, so are you in my hand."

Jeremiah 18:3–6 ESV

We are God's workmanship, created in Christ Jesus to do good works, which God prepared in advance for us to do.

Ephesians 2:10

The Room:
My Life

A bouquet of flowers brightens any room. To fully capture a bouquet's beauty and fragrance, though, you want to find the best possible place to put it. This week, think about your "room"— your life, circumstances, and opportunities. How has your Savior put you in the best possible place to honor him?

Whatever you do, do it all for the glory of God.

1 Corinthians 10:31

Blessed:
Living in Light

*For everyone who has will be given
more, and he will have an abundance.*

Matthew 25:29

Imagine you have spent the last hour or so clipping flowers in your garden. You take them inside and form two bouquets to take to friends recovering from recent illnesses.

You arrive at Sally's home and lay a bouquet in her arms. As you sit to chat, you gasp in disbelief as Sally stashes the flowers in a magazine rack in a dark corner of the room. Odd? With a bouquet of flowers, yes. But it's all too common with the blessings God gives to his beloved daughters.

False humility tempts us to play down our talents and skills. Doubt in our abilities creates fear and timidity. Ingratitude leads us to act as if God hasn't given us any gifts and talents at all.

Next, you proceed to Adele's home. Adele appears delighted with the bouquet. From her china cabinet, she chooses a lovely vase. She unwraps her flowers, arranges them, and adds water. Then she displays the flowers in the sunniest window of the room. Odd? With a bouquet of flowers, not at all. But it's all too uncommon with the blessings God gives to his beloved daughters.

What a bouquet of blessings—talents, skills, abilities, insights, and wisdom—God has given you! To all of this, he adds the blessing of healthy humility. Still, he intends that you honor, develop, and use your gifts to enhance your own life and the lives of others. The sunshine of godly confidence helps you to overcome fear and reach out to others in helpful and productive ways. The wholesome glow of gratitude praises God, the giver of every good gift, for all the blessings he has chosen to give to you.

It's unlikely you will want to present Sally with another bouquet soon. But you'll remember Adele next time you're out in your garden cutting flowers. You're likely to gather your best blooms and give them to her, not for any special occasion, but "just because."

Similarly, when you display the blessings God gives you in the Sonshine of your church, family, or community, expect your Lord to shower down an even bigger bunch of blessings tomorrow . . . and the next day . . . and the next.

Lord, help me use my gifts with confidence and godly humility for the good of others. Amen.

Blessed:
Standing Firm

Well done, good and faithful servant!
You have been faithful with a few things;
I will put you in charge of many things.
Come and share your master's happiness!

Matthew 25:23

Multiple paws reach for spikes of springy green-ery. Noses sniff big blossoms. Flower vases act like a magnet for my curious kitties. Floral arrangements at my house must find a place high, solid, and inaccessible!

The bouquet of blessings you have received from God requires special placement, too. If you set it on the low, rickety table of worldly values, you'll soon find yourself battered by the world's disapproving opinion; many in our society consider love, joy, peace, and patience old-fashioned virtues.

If you expose your bouquet of blessings to the claws of society's values, you'll find your blossoms mangled. On the other hand, self-promotion and people-pleasing behaviors will also upend the Spirit-inspired motivation to love and serve.

Because we tend to be sensitive and social by nature, it's easy for God's daughters to rely on the applause or frowns of those around us as we act and react to circumstances in our lives. But if we let our confidence rest on our feelings, we will sooner or later find our giftedness bouncing to the floor and shattering into a thousand pieces.

Worldly values, self-focus, and fluctuating feelings prowl around like a cat stalking a dangling leaf. Instead, let the Holy Spirit place you on the high, safe, and solid shelf of his love and acceptance. Jesus' love, care, and forgiveness will lift you high above the negativity of worldly values. As the Holy Spirit daily strengthens your faith through his Word of hope and promise, he will work in you the confidence and love that make it possible to use every gift God gives for the good of others.

Above all, the Holy Spirit's gift of faith will keep you blooming until the day God says to you, "Well done, good and faithful servant! You have been faithful with a few things; I will put you in charge of many things. Come and share your master's happiness!" (Matthew 25:23).

Holy Spirit, deepen my confidence in you, not in myself. Then show me how to glorify you by using the gifts and abilities you have given me to help others.
Amen.

Blessed:
Giving—and
Receiving!

*Each one should use whatever gift he
has received to serve others, faithfully
administering God's grace in its various forms.*
1 Peter 4:10

"Do not touch!" No one has left a printed sign, but
the bright, sunny floral arrangement perched on
top of an ornate pedestal clearly communicates
"eyes only." The arrangement captivates your
eyes as you circle the pedestal to take it in.

Perhaps you know a "do not touch" woman. Her
accomplishments far exceed those of anyone
else, and her energy and vibrancy command
attention wherever she goes. She's a phenomenal
giver who would do anything for you, and she has
blessed your life many times over.

You soon realize, however, that she's uncomfort-
able receiving anything from you. She's never
asked you for any kind of help or advice, and, as
far as you know, she's never asked anyone else
either. Maybe you recognize yourself as a "do not
touch" woman.

If so, you're experiencing less than the full sum of God's blessings for you. You see, you are blessed as God's Holy Spirit works *through* you. But you are also blessed as the Holy Spirit works through the lives and hearts of others *for you!*

So delight in the gifts of others. Pay special attention to "God's grace in its various forms" your friends, neighbors, co-workers, and loved ones demonstrate (1 Peter 4:10). Name their distinctive skills, abilities, and talents, and thank God for the bouquet of blessings he has given to them.

Then, trust those around you to bless you in all the ways they can. Let them minister to you as you ask the advice of mature Christians. Accept the help of someone who can help you carry a few of your burdens. Confide in trusted family members and friends. Let Jesus touch you through the gentle hands and compassionate hearts of those who love you and care about you.

Lord Jesus, send your Spirit to work in me the graciousness that receives from your people as well as gives to them. Amen.

Blessed:
Forgiving and
Being Forgiven

Forgive, and you will be forgiven.
Luke 6:37

A rose means "I love you." A rose with thorns, however, means "I am angry with you."

When you greet people and interact with them, it's as if you're handing out roses. You're extending an expression of your feelings toward them in the attitude, words, and actions you choose.

The fragrance of a rose attracts people. Perhaps you know someone whose presence seems to work like a pleasing fragrance. Her thoughts, suffused with truth, purity, and loveliness, scent her conversations with gentleness and peace. Her words, immersed in godly wisdom, permeate her actions with the aroma of authenticity and genuine love for others, the kind of love that says, "Because Jesus first loved me, I love you."

That fragrance is pleasing and delightful, comforting and joyful. It's heart lightening and day brightening. If you're giving out roses with this kind of fragrance, people want to be around you.

Thorns, however, repel others. Ill temper, criticism, and lack of forgiveness describe a prickly personality. No one wants to come too close! An on-edge, volatile temper brings tension into the room, quickly quelling the goodwill and spontaneity of others. Barbed criticism unbolts the door to intimidation, apprehension, and fear—feelings no one welcomes. Lack of forgiveness leaves windows wide open to the stench of sins that pull people apart—offense, blame, anger, grudges.

In the cross of his Son, the Master Gardener reaches into our prickly lives, bringing the peace of forgiveness. Knowing the fragrance of his love, we can come to him in hope, confessing our thorniness, naming those people to whom we have handed a thorny stem instead of a fragrant blossom. At the same time, we can recall the occasions in which we have been stabbed by the sins of others. And we can forgive that person . . . and that person . . . and yes, even that person, because Jesus has forgiven us.

Lord Jesus, I want to hand out roses—fragrant and without thorns. Work your love in me so that those around me see my life set in your love, honoring you and encouraging them. Amen.

Blessed:
Living Now
and Forever

*He died for us so that, whether we
are awake or asleep, we may live
together with him.*

1 Thessalonians 5:10

- Add a penny to the water.
- Throw in an aspirin.
- Dip the stems in boiling water.
- Put the whole thing in the refrigerator.

Ask a dozen friends how to make a bouquet of flowers last longer, and you're likely to hear a dozen different answers. No matter what method you use, however, even the most carefully kept bouquet will eventually lose its freshness, its scent, and its beauty.

That's life here on earth! Everything we know eventually suffers from the passing of time and the losses of death and decay. Only the eternal God, the God who saves in the death and resurrection of his Son, has the power and authority to give life everlasting, eternal life.

While we were helpless, Jesus entered our world of death and decay to introduce eternal life. His miracles of healing revealed his ability to make us whole, physically and spiritually. His teachings showed us his Father's will. His death on the cross in payment for our sins proved his love for us. His resurrection opened for all believers the way to life everlasting.

Because God's Spirit lives and works in you, you can see beyond the stresses of today. You see the never-ending glory of life with God, and your hope rests on the unchangeable truth of God's Word.

Similarly, you know that your true beauty consists not of the symmetry of your features, the size of your dress, or the smoothness of your skin—after all, all that will pass away. True beauty, abundant beauty, comes from your Creator, Redeemer God.

Before you close this booklet today, page through the devotions. Name the particular blessings you hold in the bouquet God has made you to be. Give thanks! Ask the Holy Spirit to help you develop his blessings and use them to honor him.

Lord Jesus, may your bouquet of blessings in my life blossom for your glory. Amen.

Placed to Praise Eternally

You [God] formed my inward parts. . . . My frame was not hidden from You. . . . Your eyes saw my substance, being yet unformed. And in Your book they all were written, The days fashioned for me, When as yet there were none of them.

Psalm 139:13–16 NKJV

Praise the LORD! I will give thanks to the LORD with my whole heart.

Psalm 111:1 ESV

I love the LORD, for he heard my voice; he heard my cry for mercy. Because he turned his ear to me, I will call on him as long as I live.

Psalm 116:1–2